Why do magnets stick to the fridge?

Disney BOOKS BY MAIL

When Mickey Wonders Why, he searches out
the answers with a little
help from these friendly experts:

DK Direct Limited

Managing Art Editor Eljay Crompton
Senior Editor Rosemary McCormick
Writer John Farndon
Illustrators The Alvin White Studios and Richard Manning
Designers Wayne Blades, Veneta Bullen, Richard Clemson,
Sarah Goodwin, Diane Klein, Sonia Whillock

Contents

Why do cakes rise when they bake?

Because the cook mixes a teaspoonful or so of baking powder into the cake mixture. When the cake is baked in the oven, the heat causes the baking powder to make lots of bubbles of carbon dioxide gas inside the cake. The bubbles blow up like balloons, making the cake bigger.

Baking bread

Yeast is another ingredient that makes things rise by creating gas bubbles. Yeast makes things rise even more than baking powder. People usually use yeast when they bake bread.

Tasty facts

Most cakes, like these cup cakes, are made with flour, sugar, eggs, and butter. Sugar makes cakes taste sweet, butter makes them moist, and eggs help to glue the ingredients together.

You don't need baking powder to make cookies. Can you guess why?

What is a shadow?

A shadow is a place where light cannot reach because something is blocking its path. Light travels in straight lines and cannot bend around things, so it stops or bounces back when it hits an object – leaving a dark gap behind in exactly the same shape as the object.

Sun time
Shadows are always on the side of the object facing away from the light source. When the light source moves, so does the shadow. Sundials can give the time because as the sun moves around during the day, so does its shadow on the sundial.

Watch that shadow
When a ground hog leaves its burrow in February, people look at its shadow to see if an early spring is on the way. If its shadow is long, there are six more weeks of winter to go. Brrrrrr!

Light laughs
Why did the teacher wear dark glasses?
Because the class was so bright!

Shadow facts

☞ All shadows have a fuzzy edge.

☞ When the moon passes between the earth and the sun, and casts its shadow on the earth, we call this a solar eclipse.

Why do cherries look red?

Colors are really colored light. So when you see red you are seeing red light. Cherries look red because daylight is all the colors of the rainbow – but the cherry skin has soaked up all the other colors, except red. So a cherry bounces only red light toward your eyes.

Important colors

If you mix the colors red, yellow, and blue together in different combinations, you can get almost any other color.

Spinning colors

When this wheel spins, the colored dots blur together to make other colors.

Colorful facts

☞ Monkeys and many kinds of birds see colors the same way people do. But some animals can't see colors at all. Scientists think that crocodiles and dogs see colors as different shades of gray. They also think that bees cannot see the color red.

Why does ice cream melt so easily?

Different things melt at different temperatures. Ice cream melts at quite a low temperature. That's because it contains solid crystals of ice. It melts easily because when it gets warm the ice turns to water. If you heated it enough, the water would turn to steam, which is tiny drops of water, leaving behind just a gooey powder.

Boiling over
When a liquid gets hotter, more and more of it turns to gas. Watch what happens to milk when it is heated in a saucepan. You will see little gas bubbles appear as it warms up.

Scientific facts

☞ Like water, most things in the world are solid when they are very cold, and melt to liquid when they get warmer. When they get very hot, they boil away to gas (like air).

☞ Liquids have no shape of their own. They take the shape of the container they are placed in.

Why does smoke rise?

Because heat makes air weigh less and so the smoke is carried upward by the hot air rising above a fire. Smoke is made of tiny specks that come from things that have been burning.

Up and away!
Did you know that birds and gliders are carried up and away by warm air currents?

Hot air facts

☞ Long ago Native Americans used smoke to send messages to each other.

☞ Ancient Romans heated their homes with hot air that flowed through passages underneath their floors and within their walls.

13

Heating up

Hot water rises just like hot air. This helps people heat their homes. Water is heated by boilers which are usually kept in the basement. The hot water travels up pipes all through the house.

Why is sunshine warm?

Sunshine is warm because the sun is boiling hot. It's as hot as billions of fires all burning at the same time. Its heat travels to us through space, in waves of energy, a little like waves in the ocean. When these waves touch us we feel the warmth of the sun.

The sun's energy
People have invented ways to use the sun's energy. Some calculators have parts that turn sunlight into electricity. If the calculators are kept in the dark, they won't work.

Inside a greenhouse
A greenhouse is nice and warm for plants because the glass traps the sun's heat inside. The layer of air around the earth is a little like the glass in a greenhouse – it keeps the earth warm.

14

Warming facts

Millions of years ago, just like today, plants used sunlight to make food. Then animals ate the plants. When these plants and animals died, their remains were buried and slowly turned into coal, oil, and gas. We call coal, oil, and gas "fossil" fuels.

Why is it hard work climbing stairs?

Because when you climb stairs, you are fighting against gravity. Gravity is the force that tugs everything toward the center of the earth. That's why things fall to the ground when they are dropped. Gravity holds us on the earth. If it wasn't for gravity, we would float off into space.

Gravity facts

☞ The British scientist Isaac Newton was the first person to understand the force of gravity.

☞ If you dropped a big stone, and a little stone, they would both fall to the ground at exactly the same speed.

Going up!
What goes up
and down
but never moves?
Stairs

Having fun
We don't always fight against gravity. Sometimes we use it to have fun. Gravity is what pulls you down a slide and helps you swing backward and forward.

Three sodas, please!
It's best to carry large objects by holding them under their center of gravity. That's the point where the weight of the object balances.

Why do magnets stick to the fridge?

Magnets are pieces of metal that stick to each other. But they also stick to other things that are made of iron and steel. They do this by turning these things into magnets, too. Magnets stick to the fridge door because they turn the metal in the door into a magnet.

Poles together

Here's a magnet experiment for you. Did you know that every magnet has two ends or "poles" – a north pole and a south pole? A north pole sticks to a south pole.

18

Magnetic facts

The ends of a magnet are called poles because the earth is a giant magnet, with one end at the north pole, and the other at the south pole. If you let a magnet swing freely, one end will point toward the north pole, and the other to the south. This is how a magnetic compass works to show you where north is.

Poles apart

Now try this experiment. If you place both magnets' south poles together, or both north poles together, they will push each other away. Try it and watch what happens.

Why are loudspeakers loud?

Sound is simply air moving. Loudspeakers make sounds bigger by shaking the air more. When music goes through a loudspeaker, large magnets inside it shake a big paper cone in time with the music. When the cone shakes, it shakes the air to make a sound just like the music – only louder!

Shaky sound
If you hold a piece of paper and shake it backward and forward, you will hear a sound. What you are hearing is the air shaking as the paper moves it.

Sound facts

 It is completely silent in space because there is no air there to shake.

 Sounds can be high like a whistle or low like the boom of a big bass drum.

 Sound travels through the air in waves, squeezing and stretching the air as it goes.

What is an echo?

It's the "instant replay" of a sound. When the sound hits a surface that is very near, it bounces off so quickly that you don't get a chance to hear it. But when you're in a large, empty place like a hall or a valley, the sound takes some time to travel back to you and you are able to hear it.

Echo sounding

Ships and submarines use echoes to "see" underwater. A special machine sends out bleeps that bounce off anything in the way. By measuring the time between the bleeps and the echo returning, people can tell how deep the sea is, and if there are any other ships, or submarines, nearby.

Sound pictures

Doctors use the echo of very high sounds to see unborn babies growing inside their mom.

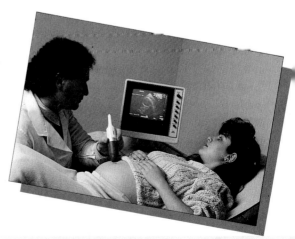

An echo, echo legend

There's a legend about a hunter who lived in a log cabin, in a place known for its echo. He didn't need an alarm clock to get up in the morning because the last thing at night, he shouted out of the window – "Time to get up!" Eight hours later the echo came back and woke him up!

Why is soda pop fizzy?

It's fizzy because the gas carbon dioxide is pumped into it. Before you open the bottle, most of the gas is trapped invisibly in the drink. But when you unscrew the top, the gas is released and forms thousands of bubbles.

Making a fizz

Why not try your own fizzy experiment? Add baking powder to water and watch what happens. When it mixes with water, it makes bubbles of carbon dioxide, too.

Built-in fizz

Some sodas are naturally fizzy. This means they make their own natural gas – like root beer.

24

Fizzy facts

☞ The very first fizzy drink was made in 1772, by a British scientist called Joseph Priestley. He hoped he'd made a medicine. He hadn't, but the drink caught on!

☞ When you breathe out, carbon dioxide is one of the gases in your breath.

Fizzy fun
What do you give a sick lemon?
Lemon-ade

25

Why do balls bounce?

Balls bounce because of their elasticity. Elasticity is a material's natural springiness. Some materials are more springy than others. When you push or pull on a springy material, it stretches, or squashes a little, then bounces back into shape. A rubber ball is so springy, first it squashes, then springs back into shape and jumps in the air.

Bouncy tires

Air is even more springy than rubber. So rubber bicycle tires are pumped full of air – and that's why you bounce when you ride over bumps!

Fun words
Why is elastic one of the longest
words in the dictionary?
Because it stretches!

Bouncy facts

☞ Inside a football is a
rubber bag filled with air.

☞ In major matches, tennis
balls are stored in a
fridge at 68°F. The cool
temperature makes the
rubber harder, and so the
balls are extra bouncy!

Can you tell what's wrong with this picture?